The Language and Sentiment of Flowers

A Romantic Dictionary

Gathered from Divers Sources
Illustrated by Vincent Perry

The C. R. Gibson Company   *Publishers*   Norwalk, Connecticut

The Language and Sentiment of Flowers

A very charming and interesting method of communicating thought is by the aid of flowers, their language and sentiment being understood by the parties who present them. Although the following list is very complete, this vocabulary may be still enlarged by the addition of other definitions, the parties having an understanding as to what language the flower shall represent. Thus an extended and sometimes important correspondence may be carried on by the presentation of bouquets, single flowers and even leaves; the charm of this interchange of thought largely consisting in the romance attendant upon an expression of sentiment in a partially disguised and hidden language.

THE LANGUAGE OF SINGLE FLOWERS

A declaration of feeling between a lady and gentleman may be expressed by single flowers, as follows:

The gentleman presents a Red Rose — "I love you." The lady admits a partial reciprocation of the sentiment by returning a Purple Pansy — "You occupy my thoughts." The gentleman presses his suit still further by an Everlasting Pea — "Wilt thou go with me?" The lady replies by a Daisy, in which she says — "I will think of it." The gentleman, in his enthusiasm, plucks and presents a Shepherd's Purse — "I offer you my all." The lady, doubtingly, returns a sprig of Laurel — "Words, though sweet, may deceive." The gentleman still affirms his declaration by a sprig of Heliotrope — "I adore you.

THE LANGUAGE OF THE BOUQUET

A collection of flowers in a bouquet may mean very much. Thus a Rose, Ivy and Myrtle will signify "Beauty, Friendship and Love." A Bachelor's Button "Hope," and a Red Rose "Love," will indicate that "I hope to obtain your love", while Jonquil and Linden mean "I desire to marry you."

So longer and shorter sentences may be readily expressed by flower-language; and by agreement, if the variety of flowers is not sufficient, a change of definition may be given the more common blossoms and plants, whereby the language and correspondence may be conducted with greater versatility.

Acacia	*Friendship*
Acacia, Yellow . .	*Secret Love*
Acanthus	*Art*
Adonis, Flos . . .	*Painful Recollections*
Agnus Castus . .	*Coldness; Life Without Love*
Agrimony	*Gratitude*
Almond	*Giddiness; Heedlessness*
Almond, Flowering . . .	*Hope*
Aloe	*Bitterness*
Amaranth	*Immortality; Unfading*
Amaryllis	*Beautiful But Timid*
Amethyst	*Admiration*
Anemone, Garden	*Forsaken; Withered Hopes; Illness*

Anemone, Windflower	· ·	*Desertion*
Angelica	· · · ·	*Inspiration*
Apple Blossom	· ·	*Preference*
Arbor Vitae	· · ·	*Unchanging Friendship*
Arbutus	· · · · ·	*Thee Only Do I Love*
Arum	· · · · · ·	*Ardor*
Ash	· · · · · ·	*Grandeur*
Aspen	· · · · ·	*Sighing*
Asphodel	· · · ·	*Remembered Beyond The Tomb*
Aster, Double German	· · · ·	*Variety*
Aster, Large Flowered	· · ·	*Afterthought; Love of Variety*

Azalea	*Temperance*
Bachelor's Button	*Hope; Single Blessedness*
Balm, Mint	*Pleasantry*
Balm of Gilead	*Healing; I Am Cured*
Balsamine	*Impatience*
Barberry	*Petulance; Ill Temper*
Basil	*Give Me Your Good Wishes*
Bay Leaf	*I Change But In Death*
Beech	*Lovers' Tryst; Prosperity*
Begonia	*Deformed*
Belladonna	*Silence*
Bindweed	*Humility; Night*
Birch	*Grace; Elegance*
Bittersweet; Nightshade	*Truth*

Blackthorn, or Sloe	*Difficulties*
Bladder Tree	*Frivolous Amusement*
Blue Bell	*Constancy*
Blue Bottle	*Delicacy*
Borage	*Abruptness*
Box	*Stoicism*
Briers	*Envy*
Broom	*Neatness: Humility*
Bryony, Black	*Be My Support*
Buckbean	*Calmness; Repose*
Bugloss	*Falsehood*
Bulrush	*Docility*
Burdock	*Touch Me Not; Importunity*
Buttercup	*Riches; Memories of Childhood*
Cabbage	*Profit*

Cactus	*Warmth*
Calla	*Delicacy; Modesty*
Camellia	*Gratitude; Perfect Loveliness*
Camomile	*Energy In Adversity*
Candytuft	*Indifference; Architecture*
Canterbury Bell	*Constancy*
Cape Jasmine	*I Am Overjoyed*
Cardinal Flower	*Distinction; Preferment*
Carnation	*Pure And Deep Love*
Cedar Leaf	*I Live For Thee*
Celandine, Lesser	*Joys To Come*

Clover, White	*I Promise*
Cockle	*Vain Is Beauty Without Merit*
Cockscomb	*Foppery*
Coltsfoot	*Justice Shall Be Done You*
Columbine, Red	*Anxious And Trembling*
Convolvulus	*Bonds*
Coreopsis	*Always Cheerful*
Coriander	*Hidden Merit*
Corn	*Riches; Abundance*
Cornelian, Cherry	*Continuance; Duration*
Cowslip	*Native Grace; Pensiveness*
Cresses	*Stability*
Crocus	*Cheerfulness*
Crowfoot	*Ingratitude*

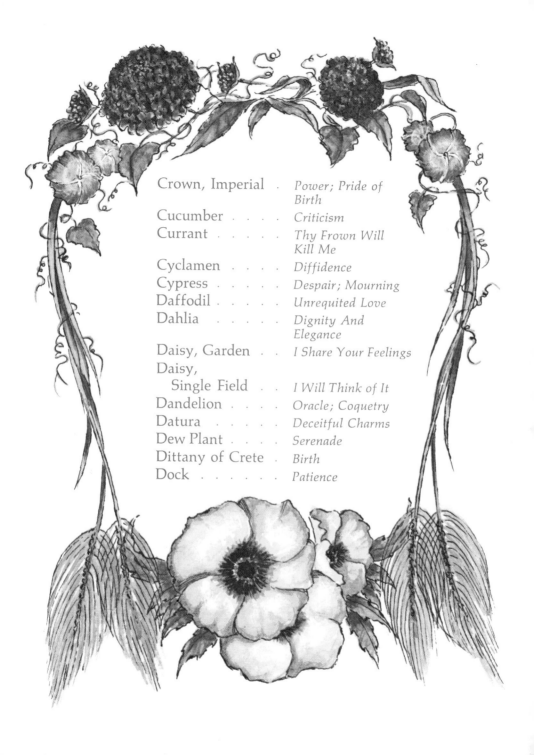

Crown, Imperial	*Power; Pride of Birth*
Cucumber	*Criticism*
Currant	*Thy Frown Will Kill Me*
Cyclamen	*Diffidence*
Cypress	*Despair; Mourning*
Daffodil	*Unrequited Love*
Dahlia	*Dignity And Elegance*
Daisy, Garden	*I Share Your Feelings*
Daisy, Single Field	*I Will Think of It*
Dandelion	*Oracle; Coquetry*
Datura	*Deceitful Charms*
Dew Plant	*Serenade*
Dittany of Crete	*Birth*
Dock	*Patience*

Dodder	*Meanness; Baseness*
Ebony Tree	*Blackness*
Eglantine	*Poetry; I Wound To Heal*
Elder	*Compassion*
Elecampane	*Tears*
Everlasting	*Always Remembered*
Everlasting Pea	*Wilt Thou Go With Me?*
Fennel	*Force; Strength*
Fern	*Sincerity*
Fir	*Elevation*
Flax	*I Feel Your Benefits*
Flos, Adonis	*Painful Recollections*
Forget-Me-Not	*Do Not Forget*
Foxglove	*Insincerity; Occupation*
Fraxinella	*Fire*

Fuchsia	*Taste; Frugality*
Gentian	*Intrinsic Worth*
Geranium, Ivy . .	*I Engage You For The Next Dance*
Geranium, Oak . .	*A Melancholy Mind*
Geranium, Rose .	*I Prefer You*
Geranium, Scarlet	*Silliness*
Gillyflower, Common . . .	*Lasting Beauty*
Gillyflower, Stock	*Promptness*
Gladiolus	*Ready Armed*
Goats' Rue . . .	*Reason*
Gold Basket . . .	*Tranquillity*
Golden Rod . . .	*Encouragement*
Gooseberry . . .	*Anticipation*
Gorse, or Turze . .	*Anger*

Grape Vine . . .	*Intemperance*
Grass	*Utility; Submission*
Greek Valerian . .	*Rupture*
Harebell	*Retirement; Grief*
Hawthorn . . .	*Hope*
Hazel	*Reconciliation*
Heath	*Solitude*
Heliotrope . . .	*I Adore You;* *Devotion*
Hellebore . . .	*Scandal*
Henbane . . .	*Blemish; Fault*
Hibiscus	*Delicate Beauty*
Hoarhound . . .	*Fire*
Holly	*Am I Forgotten;* *Foresight*
Hollyhock . . .	*Fecundity; Ambition*
Honey Flower . .	*Sweet And Secret* *Love*

Honeysuckle . . .	*Devoted Love; Fidelity*
Hop	*Injustice*
Hornbean	*Ornament*
Horse Chestnut .	*Luxury*
Houseleek	*Domestic Economy*
Houstania	*Innocence; Content*
Hyacinth	*Constancy; Benevolence*
Hydrangea . . .	*Vain-Glory; Heartlessness*
Ice Plant	*Your Looks Freeze Me*
Indian Plum . . .	*Privation*
Iris, Common Garden	*A Message For Thee*
Iris, German . . .	*Flame*

Ivy	*Friendship; Marriage*
Jasmine, Cape . .	*I Am Overjoyed*
Jasmine, White . .	*Amiability*
Jasmine, Yellow .	*Grace And Elegance*
Jonquil	*Desire; Affection Returned*
Juniper	*Asylum; Aid; Protection*
Laburnum	*Pensive Beauty*
Lady's Slipper . .	*Capricious Beauty*
Lantana	*Vigor*
Larch	*Boldness; Audacity*
Larkspur, Pink . .	*Lightness; Fickleness*
Laurel, American .	*Words, Though Sweet, May Deceive*
Laurel, Mountain .	*Glory; Victory; Ambition*

Laurestine	*I Die If Neglected*
Lavatera	*Sweet Disposition*
Lavender	*Mistrust*
Lemon Blossom	*Prudence; Discretion*
Lesser Celandine	*Joys To Come*
Lettuce	*Cold Hearted; Coolness*
Lichen	*Dejection*
Lilac, Purple	*First Emotions Of Love*
Lilac, White	*Youth*
Lily, Day	*Coquetry*
Lily Of The Valley	*Return Of Happiness*
Lily, Water	*Eloquence*
Lily, White	*Majesty; Purity*
Linden, or Lime	*Conjugal; Marriage*

Liverwort	*Confidence*
Locust Tree,	*Love Beyond*
Green	*The Grave*
Lotus Leaf	*Recantation*
Lucern	*Life*
Lupine	*Imagination*
Madder	*Calumny*
Magnolia	*Love Of Nature*
Maiden Hair . . .	*Discretion*
Manchineel Tree .	*Falseness*
Mandrake	*Rarity*
Maple	*Reserve*
Marigold	*Sacred Affection*
Marigold and	
Cypress	*Despair*
Marigold, Garden .	*Grief; Chagrin*
Marigold, Rainy .	*A Storm*

Marjoram	*Blushes*
Marshmallow . .	*Beneficence*
Marvel of Peru . .	*Timidity*
Mayflower . . .	*Welcome*
Meadow Saffron .	*My Best Days Are Past*
Mezereon	*Desire To Please*
Mignonette . . .	*Your Qualities Surpass Your Charms*
Milfoil	*War*
Milkweed	*Hope In Misery*
Mint	*Virtue*
Mistletoe	*I Surmount Everything*
Mock Orange . .	*Counterfeit; Uncertainty*

Monkshood · · ·	*Treachery;* *A Foe Is Near*
Morning Glory · ·	*Coquetry;* *Affectation*
Moss · · · · ·	*Maternal Love*
Motherwort · · ·	*Hidden Love*
Mountain Ash · ·	*I Watch Over You*
Mountain Pink · ·	*Aspiring*
Mourning Bride ·	*I Have Lost All*
Mugwort · · · ·	*Good Luck;* *Happiness*
Mulberry, Black ·	*I Shall Not* *Survive You*
Mulberry, White ·	*Wisdom*
Mullein · · · ·	*Good Nature*
Mushroom · · ·	*Suspicion*
Musk Plant · · ·	*Weakness*
Myrrh · · · · ·	*Gladness*
Myrtle · · · · ·	*Love In Absence*

Narcissus	*Egotism; Self-Love*
Nasturtium . . .	*Patriotism; Splendor*
Nettle	*Cruelty*
Nightshade . . .	*Dark Thoughts; Sorcery*
Oak	*Hospitality; Bravery*
Oleander	*Beware*
Olive	*Peace*
Orange Flower . .	*Chastity*
Orchis, Bee . . .	*Error*
Orchis, Spider . .	*Skill*
Osier	*Frankness*
Osmunda	*Reverie*
Pansy, Purple . .	*You Occupy My Thoughts*
Parsley	*Festivity; Banquet*
Passion Flower . .	*Devotion; Religious Fervor*

Peach Blossom	*I Am Your Captive*
Peony	*Ostentation; Anger*
Persimmon	*Bury Me Amid Nature's Beauties*
Peppermint	*Warmth Of Feeling*
Pennyroyal	*Flee Away*
Periwinkle	*Sweet Memories*
Phlox	*Our Hearts Are United*
Pimpernel	*Rendezvous; Change*
Pine	*Endurance; Daring*
Pineapple	*You Are Perfect*
Pink, Mountain	*Aspiring*
Pink, Red	*Pure Love*

Plane, or Platane	*Genius*
Plum Tree	*Keep Your Promises*
Plum, Wild	*Independence*
Polyanthus	*Heart's Mystery*
Pomegranate	*Conceit*
Poplar, Black	*Courage*
Poplar, White	*Time*
Poppy, Red	*Consolation*
Poppy, White	*Sleep; Oblivion*
Potato	*Benevolence*
Primrose	*Modest Worth; Silent Love*
Privet, or Prim	*Prohibition*
Purple Scabious	*Mourning*
Queen Of The Meadow	*Uselessness*
Quince	*Temptation*

Ranunculus, Garden	*You Are Radiant With Charms*
Reeds	*Music*
Restharrow . . .	*Obstacle*
Rhododendron . .	*Agitation*
Rhubarb	*Advice*
Rose, Austrian . .	*Thou Art All That Is Lovely*
Rosebud, Moss . .	*Confession Of Love*
Rosebud, White .	*Too Young To Love*
Rose, China . . .	*Beauty Ever New*
Rose, Cinnamon .	*Without Pretension*
Rose, Hundred Leaved	*The Graces*
Rose Leaf	*I Never Trouble*
Rose, Moss . . .	*Superior Merit; Voluptuousness*
Rose, Musk . . .	*Capricious Beauty*
Rose, Red	*I Love You*

Rose, White . . .	*Silence*
Rose, Wild Single .	*Simplicity*
Rose, Yellow . . .	*Infidelity; Unfaithfulness*
Rosemary	*Remembrance; Your Presence Revives Me*
Rue	*Disdain*
Rush	*Docility*
Saffron, Crocus .	*Do Not Abuse Me*
Saffron, Meadow .	*My Best Days Are Past*
Sage	*Domestic Virtue; Esteem*
St. Johns' Wort .	*Animosity*
Sardonia	*Irony*
Satin Flower . . .	*Forgetfulness*
Scotch Thistle . .	*Retaliation*
Scratch Weed . .	*Roughness*

Sensitive Plant	Sensitiveness; Modesty
Serpent Cactus	Horror
Service Tree, or Sorb	Prudence
Shepherd's Purse	I Offer You My All
Silver Weed	Naivete
Snapdragon	Presumption
Snowball	Goodness
Snowdrop	Consolation; A Friend In Adversity
Sorrel	Parental Affection
Speedwell	Fidelity
Spindle Tree	Your Charms Are Graven On My Heart
Star of Bethlehem	Reconciliation; Purity

Straw	*Agreement; United*
Strawberry . . .	*Perfect Excellence*
Straw, Broken . .	*Quarrel*
Stock	*Lasting Beauty*
Sumach	*Splendid Misery*
Sunflower	*False Riches*
Sunflower, Dwarf	*Adoration*
Sunflower, Tall . .	*Lofty And Wise Thoughts*
Sweet Flag	*Fitness*
Sweet Pea	*A Meeting*
Sweet Sultan . .	*Happiness*
Sweet William . .	*Gallantry; Finesse; Dexterity*
Sycamore	*Curiosity*
Syringa	*Memory; Fraternal Love*

Tare	*Vice*
Teasel	*Misanthropy*
Thistle	*Austerity*
Thorn Apple	*Disguise*
Thrift	*Sympathy*
Thyme	*Activity*
Tremella	*Resistance*
Tuberose	*Dangerous Pleasure; Voluptuousness; Sweet Voice*
Tulip, Red	*Declaration Of Love*
Tulip, Variegated	*Beautiful Eyes*
Valerian	*Facility*
Valerian, Common	*Accommodating Disposition*

Venus's Looking
  Glass . . . . .   *Flattery*
Verbena . . . . .   *Sensibility;*
      Sensitiveness
Verbena, Purple .   *I Weep For You;*
      Regret
Verbena, White .   *Pray For Me*
Vernal Grass . . .   *Poor, But Happy*
Vervain . . . . .   *Enchantment*
Vetch . . . . . .   *I Cling To Thee*
Violet, Blue . . .   *Faithfulness*
Violet, White . .   *Purity; Candor;*
      Modesty
Volkamenia . . .   *May You Be Happy*
Wallflower . . .   *Fidelity In*
      Misfortune

Weeping Willow	*Melancholy*
Wheat	*Wealth*
Whortleberry	*Treachery*
Willow, Common	*Forsaken*
Willow, Herb	*Pretension*
Woodbine	*Fraternal Love*
Wood Sorrel	*Joy*
Wormwood	*Absence*
Yarrow	*Cure For The Heartache*
Yew	*Sadness*
Zinnia	*I Mourn Your Absence*

A Dictionary of Sentiment

Aspiring . . . Mountain Pink
Asylum . . . . Juniper
Audacity . . . Larch
Austerity . . . Thistle

Abruptness . . Borage
Absence . . . Wormwood
Accommodating Common
  Disposition . Valerian
Activity . . . . Thyme
Admiration . . Amethyst
Adoration . . . Dwarf
  Sunflower
Advice . . . . Rhubarb
Affectation . . Morning Glory
Affection
  Returned . . Jonquil
Afterthought . . China Aster
Age . . . . . Guelder Rose
Agitation . . . Rhododendron
Agreement . . . Straw
Always Cheerful . Coreopsis
Always
  Remembered . Everlasting
Ambition . . . Hollyhock,
  Mountain Laurel
Amiability . . . Jasmine
Am I Forgotten . Holly
Anger . . . . Gorse
Animosity . . . St. John's Wort
Anticipation . . Gooseberry
Anxious and
  Trembling . . Red Columbine
Ardor . . . . Arum
Art . . . . . Acanthus

Baseness . . . Dodder
Beautiful But
  Timid . . . Amaryllis
Beautiful Eyes . Variegated Tulip
Beauty Always
  New . . . . China Rose
Beauty,
  Capricious . . Lady's Slipper,
  Musk Rose
Beauty,
  Delicate . . . Hibiscus
Beauty, Mental . Clematis
Beauty, Pensive . Laburnum
Beloved
  Daughter . . Cinquefoil
Be Mine . . . . Four-Leaved
  Clover
Be My Support . Black Bryony
Beneficence . . Marshmallow
Benevolence . . Potato
Beware . . . . Oleander
Birth . . . . . Dittany of Crete
Bitterness . . . Aloe
Blackness . . . Ebony Tree
Blemish . . . . Henbane

Blushes	Marjoram
Boldness	Larch
Bonds	Convolvulus
Bravery	Oak
Bury Me Amid Nature's Beauties	Persimmon

Calmness	Buckbean
Calumny	Madder
Change	Pimpernel
Chastity	Orange Flower
Cheerfulness	Crocus
Coldheartedness	Lettuce
Coldness	Agnus Castus
Compassion	Elder
Conceit	Pomegranate
Confession of Love	Moss Rosebud
Confidence	Liverwort
Confidence in Heaven	Flowering Reed
Conjugal Love	Lime, or Linden Tree
Consolation	Red Poppy, Snowdrop
Constancy	Blue Bell, Canterbury Bell, Hyacinth
Content	Houstania
Continuance	Cherry Cornelian
Coquetry	Morning Glory, Day Lily
Counterfeit	Mock Orange
Courage	Black Poplar

Criticism	Cucumber
Cruelty	Nettle
Cure For Heartache	Yarrow
Curiosity	Sycamore

Dangerous Pleasures	Tuberose
Daring	Pine
Dark Thoughts	Nightshade
Deceitful Charms	Datura
Declaration of Love	Red Tulip
Deformed	Begonia
Dejection	Lichen, Lupine
Delicacy	Bluebottle, Calla
Desertion	Anemone, Windflower
Desire	Jonquil
Desire to Please	Mezereon
Despair	Cypress
Devoted Love	Honeysuckle
Devotion	Heliotrope, Passion Flower
Difficulty	Blackthorn
Diffidence	Cyclamen
Discretion	Lemon Blossom, Maiden Hair
Disdain	Rue
Disguise	Thorn Apple
Docility	Rush
Do Me Justice	Chestnut
Domestic Economy	Houseleek

Domestic Virtue	*Sage*
Do Not Abuse Me	*Saffron, Crocus*
Do Not Forget	*Forget-Me-Not*
Duration	*Cherry Cornelian*

Egotism	*Narcissus*
Elevation	*Fir*
Eloquence	*Water Lily*
Enchantment	*Vervain*
Encouragement	*Goldenrod*
Endurance	*Pine*
Energy in Adversity	*Camomile*
Envy	*Brier*
Error	*Bee Orchis*
Esteem	*Garden Sage*
Excellence	*Camellia*

Facility	*Valerian*
Faithfulness	*Blue Violet*
Falsehood	*Burgloss*
Falseness	*Manchineel Tree*
False Riches	*Sunflower*
Fecundity	*Hollyhock*
Festivity	*Parsley*
Fickleness	*Pink Larkspur*
Fidelity	*Honeysuckle, Speedwell*

Fidelity in Misfortune	*Wallflower*
Fire	*Fraxinella, Hoarhound*
First Emotions of Love	*Purple Lilac*
Fitness	*Sweet Flag*
Flame	*Iris*
Flattery	*Venus's Looking Glass*
Flee Away	*Pennyroyal*
Foppery	*Cockscomb*
Force	*Fennel*
Foresight	*Holly*
Forgetfulness	*Satin Flower*
Forget Me Not	*Forget-Me-Not*
Forgiveness	*Cinnamon*
Frankness	*Osier*
Fraternal Love	*Woodbine*
Friend In Adversity	*Snowdrop*
Friendship	*Rose, Acacia, Ivy*
Friendship, Unchanging	*Arbor Vitae*
Frivolous Amusement	*Bladder Tree*
Frugality	*Chiccory, Fuchsia*

Gallantry	*Sweet William*
Genius	*Plane Tree*
Giddiness	*Almond*
Give Me Your Good Wishes	*Basil*

Gladness . . .	*Myrrh*
Glory	*Laurel*
Good	
Education . .	*Cherry*
Good Luck . .	*Mugwort*
Good Nature . .	*Mullein*
Goodness . . .	*Snowball*
Grace	*Birch, Hundred Leaved Rose*
Graces	*Hundred Leaved Rose*
Grace and Elegance . . .	*Yellow Jasmine*
Grandeur . . .	*Ash Tree*
Gratitude . . .	*Agrimony, Camellia*
Grief	*Harebell, Marigold*

(decorated initial H)

Happiness . . .	*Mugwort, Sweet Sultan*
Healing	*Balm of Gilead*
Heart Left To Desolation . .	*Chrysanthemum*
Heartlessness . .	*Hydrangea*
Heart's Mystery .	*Polyanthus*
Hidden Love . .	*Motherwort*
Hidden Merit . .	*Coriander*
Hidden Worth .	*Coriander*
Hope	*Bachelor's Button, Flowering Almond, Hawthorn*
Hope In Misery .	*Milk Weed*

Horror	*Dragonwort, Serpent Cactus*
Hospitality . .	*Oak*
Humility . . .	*Broom, Small Bindweed*

(decorated initial I)

I Adore You . .	*Heliotrope*
I Am Overjoyed . .	*Cape Jasmine*
I Am Your Captive . . .	*Peach Blossom*
I Change But In Death . .	*Bay Leaf*
I Cling To Thee .	*Vetch*
I Die If Neglected . .	*Laurestina*
I Engage You For The Next Dance . . .	*Ivy Geranium*
I Feel Your Kindness . .	*Flax*
I Have Lost All .	*Mourning Bride*
I Live For Thee .	*Cedar Leaf*
I Love You . . .	*Red Rose*
Imagination . .	*Lupine*
Immortality . .	*Amaranth*
I Mourn Your Absence .	*Zinnia*
Impatience . . .	*Balsamine*
Independence . .	*Wild Plum Tree*
Indifference . .	*Everflowering Candytuft*
Industry . . .	*Red Clover*
I Never Trouble . . .	*Rose Leaf*

Infidelity . . . Yellow Rose
Ingratitude . . Crowfoot
Injustice . . . Hop
Innocence . . . Houstania
Insincerity . . . Foxglove
Inspiration . . Angelica
Intemperance . Grape Vine
Intrinsic Worth . Gentian
I Offer You
   My All . . . Shepherd's Purse
I Prefer You . . Rose Geranium
I Promise . . White Clover
Irony . . . . Sardonia
I Share Your
   Feelings . . . Garden Daisy
I Watch Over
   You . . . Mountain Ash
I Weep For You . Purple Verbena
I Will Think
   Of It . . . . Field Daisy

Lasting Beauty . Common
             Gillyflower,
             Stock
Life . . . . . Lucern
Life Without
   Love . . . . Agnus Castus
Lightness . . . Larkspur
Lofty And Wise
   Thoughts . . Tall Sunflower
Love . . . . Arbutus,
             Rose
Love Beyond   Green Locust
   The Grave . . Tree
Love In
   Absence . . . Myrtle
Love Of Variety China Aster
Lover Of
   Nature . . . Magnolia
Lovers Tryst . . Beech
Luxury . . . Chestnut Tree

Joy . . . . . Wood Sorrel
Joys To Come Lesser Celandine
Justice Shall Be
   Done To You . Coltsfoot

Majesty . . . White, Lily
Marriage . . . Ivy
Maternal Love . Moss
Matrimony . . American Linden
May You Be
   Happy . . . Volkamenia
Meanness . . . Dodder
Meeting . . . Sweet Pea

Keep Your
   Promises . . Plum Tree

Melancholy . .	*Weeping Willow*
Melancholy	
Mind	*Oak Geranium*
Memories Of	
Childhood . .	*Buttercup*
Memory . . .	*Syringa*
Mental Beauty .	*Clematis*
Message . . .	*Iris*
Misanthropy . .	*Teasel*
Mistrust . . .	*Lavender*
Modest Works .	*Primrose*
Modesty . . .	*Calla, Violet*
Modesty And	
Purity . . .	*White Lily*
Mourning . . .	*Cypress, Purple*
	Scabious
Music	*Reed*
My Best Days	
Are Past . . .	*Meadow Saffron*

Naivete	*Silverweed*
Native Grace . .	*Cowslip*
Neatness . . .	*Broom*

Obstacle . . .	*Restharrow*
Oracle . . .	*Dandelion*
Ostentation . .	*Peony*
Our Hearts Are	
United . . .	*Phlox*

Painful	
Recollections .	*Flos Adonis*
Parental	
Affection . .	*Sorrel*
Patriotism . . .	*Nasturtium*
Peace	*Olive*
Pensive	
Beauty . . .	*Laburnum*
Pensiveness . .	*Cowslip*
Perfect	
Loveliness . .	*Camellia*
Perfect	
Excellence . .	*Strawberry*
Petulance . . .	*Barberry*
Pleasantry . . .	*Mint Balm*
Poetry	*Eglantine*
Poor But	
Happy . . .	*Vernal Grass*
Power	*Crown Imperial*
Pray For Me . .	*White Verbena*
Preference . . .	*Apple Blossom,*
	Cardinal Flower
Presumption . .	*Snapdragon*
Pretension . . .	*Spiked Willow*
	Herb
Privation . . .	*Indian Plum*
Profit	*Cabbage*
Prohibition . .	*Privet*
Promptness . .	*Stock,*
	Gillyflower
Prosperity . . .	*Beech*
Protection . . .	*Juniper*
Prudence . . .	*Lemon Blossom,*
	Service Tree
	(Sorb)

Pure And
  Deep Love . . . Carnation
Pure And
  Lovely . . . . Red Rosebud
Purity . . . . White Lily,
  White Violet,
  Star of
  Bethlehem

Quarrel . . . . Broken Straw

Rarity . . . . Mandrake
Ready Armed . Gladiolus
Reason . . . . Goat's Rue
Recantation . . Lotus Leaf
Reconciliation . Hazel,
  Star of
  Bethlehem
Relief . . . . Balm of Gilead
Religious
  Fervor . . . Passion Flower
Remembered
  Beyond The
  Tomb . . . . Asphodel
Remembrance . Rosemary
Rendezvous . . Maple,
  Pimpernel,
  Chickweed
Reserve . . . . Maple

Resistance . . . Tremella
Retaliation . . . Scotch Thistle
Retirement . . Harebell
Return Of Lily of The
  Happiness . . Valley
Reverie . . . . Osmunda
Riches . . . . Buttercup, Corn
Rigour . . . . Lantana
Roughness . . . Scratchweed
Rupture . . . . Greek Valerian
Rural
  Happiness . . Yellow Violet

Sacred
  Affection . . Marigold
Sadness . . . . Yew
Scandal . . . . Hellebore
Sensibility . . . Verbena
Sensitiveness . . Sensitive Plant
Serenade . . . Dew Plant
Sighing . . . . Aspen Tree
Silence . . . . White Rose,
  Belladonna
Silent Love . . Primrose
Silliness . . . . Scarlet Geranium
Simplicity . . . Single Wild Rose
Single Bachelor's
  Blessedness . Button
Skill . . . . . Spider Orchis
Sleep . . . . . White Poppy
Slighted Love . . Yellow
  Chrysanthemum
Solitude . . . . Heath
Splendid Misery . Sumach
Stability . . . Cress

Stoicism . . .	*Box Tree*
Storm	*Rainy Marigold*
Strength . . .	*Fennel*
Submission . .	*Grass*
Succour . . .	*Juniper*
Superior Worth .	*Moss Rose*
Surety	*Cistus*
Suspicion . . .	*Mushroom*
Sweet And	
Secret Love .	*Honey Flower*
Sweet	
Disposition .	*Lavatera*
Sweet	
Memories . .	*Periwinkle*
Sympathy . . .	*Thrift*

Taste	*Scarlet Fuchsia*
Tears	*Elecampane*
Temperance . .	*Azalea*
Temptation . .	*Quince*
Thankfulness . .	*Agrimony*
Thee Only Do	
I Love . . .	*Arbutus*
Thou Art All	
That Is Lovely	*Austrian Rose*
Thoughts . . .	*Pansy*
Thy Frown Will	
Kill Me . . .	*Currant*
Ties	*Tendrils of*
	Climbing Plants
Time	*White Poplar*
Timidity . . .	*Marvel of Peru*
Too Young	
To Love . . .	*White Rosebud*

Touch Me Not .	*Burdock*
Tranquillity . .	*Gold Basket*
Transient	*Night-Blooming*
Beauty . . .	*Cereus*
Treachery . . .	*Monkshood*
Truth	*Bittersweet;*
	Nightshade

Unchanging	
Friendship . .	*Arbor Vitae*
Unfortunate	
Love	*Scabious*
Union	*White Straw*
Unity	*White and Red*
	Rose Together
Unrequited	
Love	*Daffodil*
Uselessness . .	*Queen Of The*
	Meadow
Utility	*Grass*

Vain Is Beauty	
Without Merit	*Cockle*
Variety	*China Aster*
Vice	*Tare*
Virtue	*Mint*
Virtue	
Domestic . .	*Sage*

War . . . . . *Milfoil*
Warmth of
   Feeling . . . *Peppermint*
Weakness . . . *Musk Plant*
Wealth . . . *Wheat*
Welcome . . . *Mayflower*
Wilt Thou Go
   With Me . . *Everlasting Pea*
Wisdom . . . *White Mulberry*
Withered Hopes . *Garden Anemone*
Without
   Pretension . . *Cinnamon Rose*
Words Though
   Sweet May
   Deceive . . . *Laurel*

You Are Perfect . *Pineapple*
You Are Radiant
   With Charms . *Ranunculus*
You Occupy
   My Thoughts . *Purple Pansy*
Your Charms
   Are Engraven
   On My Heart . *Spindle Tree*
Your Looks
   Freeze Me . . *Ice Plant*
Your Qualities
   Surpass Your
   Charms . . . *Mignonette*
Youth . . . . *White Lilac*

Borage
Abruptness

Larch
Boldness

Pine
Daring

Vervain
Enchantment

Purple Lilac
First emotions of love

Basil
Give me your good wishes

Bachelor's Button
Hope

Love at First Sight.

June 1, 1890

DEAR MISS HAWLEY:

You will, I trust, forgive this abrupt and plainly spoken letter. Although I have been in your company but once, I cannot forbear writing to you in defiance of all rules of etiquette. Affection is sometimes of slow growth, but sometimes it springs up in a moment. I left you last night with my heart no longer my own. I cannot, of course, hope that I have created any interest in you, but will you do me the great favor to allow me to cultivate your acquaintance? Hoping that you may regard me favorably, I shall await with much anxiety your reply. I remain,

Yours Devotedly,

BENSON GOODRICH.

Rose
Love

Purple Pansy
You occupy my thoughts

Heliotrope
Devotion

A Favorable Reply.

June 6, 1890

Mr. Goodrich.

Dear Sir: Undoubtedly I ought to call you severely to account for your declaration of love at first sight, but I really cannot find it in my heart to do so, as I must confess that, after our brief interview last evening, I have thought much more of you than I should have been willing to have acknowledged had you not come to the confession first. Seriously speaking, we know but very little of each other yet, and we must be very careful not to exchange our hearts in the dark. I shall be happy to receive you here, as a friend, with a view to our further acquaintance. I remain, dear sir,

MARION HAWLEY.

Goldenrod
Encouragement

Garden Sage
Esteem

Osier
Frankness

Jonquil
Affection returned

Garden Daisy
I share your feelings

Sweet Pea
Meeting

Lemon Blossom
Prudence

Peppermint
Warmth of feeling

Pansy
Thought

Periwinkle
Sweet Memories